It's your move!

...for anyone moving on to secondary school

Scripture Union

"Everything seemed to be so much bigger than my last school. There were hundreds of boys, the school hall was enormous and I'm sure the teachers looked larger too! I was very fortunate because I had a friend who had been there for a year. Having a friend made all the difference!"
Brian Ogden, author

"On my first day at secondary school, I remember (with acute embarrassment) the first PE lesson. My mother, for reasons best known to herself, had put a seam up the middle of my gym skirt, thinking it was supposed to be a pair of shorts. I couldn't get them onto my legs and had to do the whole lesson (horror of horrors!) in my knickers!"
Moira Kean, BBC Producer

"There was a rumour that on the first day some new boys were put in the school dustbins. I spent the day in terror, fearing that I would end up in the bin. What a relief when the final bell went!"
Brian Sears, football statistician

Scripture Union, 207–209 Queensway, Bletchley, MK2 2EB, England.

© Scripture Union, 2000.

ISBN 1 85999 501 2

The right of Nick Harding to be identified as author of pp6-16 has been asserted by him in accordance with the Copyright, Designs and Patents Act 1988.

British Library Cataloguing-in-Publication Data

A catalogue record for this book is available from the British Library.

Cover design by David Lund Design.
Internal design by David Lund Design.

Printed and bound in Malta by Interprint

Scripture quotations are from the Contemporary English Version © American Bible Society 1991, 1992, 1995. Used by permission/Anglicisations © British & Foreign Bible Society 1997.

With special thanks to Tim Cutting and the Moving On Up Schools Education team of the Bridgebuilder Trust. Also to Nick Jeffery, Schools and Resources Youth Worker, Bristol.

This book
was given to

by

in preparation for secondary school

Date

My personal profile

Name

Date of birth

Height (without heels!)

Primary school

Favourite subject

Favourite teacher

Best friends

Secondary school

Form tutor

First day of term

Collect the signatures of people you want to **remember!**

A-Z
Survival Guide

Arguments

Moving schools can be a stressful time, so you are quite likely to lose your temper or get irritable. You may argue with your parents about your school uniform, or with old friends at school who are not spending so much time with you. If you're getting wound up, count to ten before you say anything, or walk away.

Assemblies

Like them or hate them, assemblies have to happen! In your new school they will probably be shorter and less fun. Some assemblies will include prayers or times of quiet. Use that opportunity to think about what was said and to think quietly or maybe pray for yourself and others.

Boys

There could be plenty of new boys to get to know and if you're a girl (and not going to a girls-only school!) that might be good or bad news! Some boys want to show off and many will seem immature. But others will be worth getting to know as friends. It's not worth trying to get a boyfriend too quickly – having lots of friends is much more fun!

Books

There are plenty of books and some will be great! The school library is a good place for homework or finding out information. Try to read what you need for each lesson and find good books that'll help with your studies and your life.

Idea: You might even want to see if the world's bestselling book has anything to say! (See page 63 to find out what it is.)

Bullying

Bullies are weak people. There's no excuse for bullying. If you think you're being bullied, don't let it go on. Tell a teacher, or someone else you can trust, immediately. That's the brave way to deal with cowards. Page 25 gives you some wise advice on this!

Break

A great time to let off steam, but takes some getting used to in a larger school. Try to stick with friends and stay in one place for a few days, until you feel confident to move around and mix a bit.

Brothers and sisters in school

If you have a brother or sister who is already at your new school, it can either be great, or pretty embarrassing! Teachers may read the list of names in the class and ask, "You're not related to HIM/HER, are you?" in a worried tone! They may expect you to be the super-human creep that he or she is. Don't worry – just be you, not anyone else.

Canteen

Moving to secondary school can mean you have a better choice of food at lunchtime. But when loads of young people get together to eat, it can be very noisy. If you use the dining room, watch what everyone else does. And try not to drop your tray on the first day!

Choices

You will have to make choices about many different things, including the friends you have, clubs you join, sports you play, or even the kind of lunch you eat! Later, you will have to choose subjects which could affect your future. Of course, there are also important choices to do with right and wrong. To make choices you need guidance, so talk to teachers, parents and friends. Many people ask God to help them make the right decisions.

Clubs

There will be plenty of clubs at your new school – chances to play more sport, make music or develop other interests. Make the most of these opportunities, but don't take on too much. You'll need time and energy for your home life and social life. Some schools have a Christian Union, which is a lunchtime or after-school club where young people go to find out more about God. You may think the CU is going to be boring or full of odd people. You may be wrong, but you'll never really know until you try!

Detention

Some schools keep students in at lunchtime or after school if they forget homework or break school rules. Detention is a waste of everyone's time, so it's best to keep out of it. If you do end up in detention, try to behave, or you'll end up in another one.

Drinks machine

There's a knack to using one! Watch someone else use it, and then copy exactly what they did. If the machine eats your money, make sure you know how to get it back (but no kicking!).

Drugs

Illegal drugs are bad news. There may be a few students who want to persuade others to use drugs. They are always expensive and always harmful. It may be tempting to experiment, but drugs can cause illness and brain damage and cause users to lose control of themselves. If you come across them at school, walk away and report it – you'll be saving others from pain as well as yourself.

English

Language and literature courses cover how we speak and write the language. Some plays and novels may seem dull, but give them a chance. You might just find something you like. If you're really getting stuck with a book or a play you've got to study, why not see if there's a film made of it that you could watch?

Finding your way

Even if you do get lost, it's not the end of the world. Use the map of the school even if it is confusing! By the end of the first week, you'll know your way around. Always ask someone where you should go, rather than stumbling into a class of cool Year 10s! And try not to get separated from others in your class. Then you can all get lost together!

Form tutor

This is the teacher who checks the register and deals with any problems. Form tutors are usually chosen carefully because they are approachable and helpful. Don't be afraid to tell them if things are going wrong or if you feel bad about your first days at the school. They really are there to help.

Friends

If your friends are not going to the same school, you may feel a bit lost and lonely. But you won't be the only one. And friends from your old school may suddenly decide they've had enough of you as a friend! Very soon you'll probably find someone who has got things in common with you and a new friendship begins. If you make the effort to talk to others who seem to be on their own, you will find yourself making friends. Write a list of new friends after two weeks and see how well you have done.

Girls

Being in larger, mixed schools usually brings boys into contact with more girls. That can seem wonderful for boys! Often, however, most of the girls in the school will be older than you and most will not want to have anything to do with you. Try to get to know girls as friends and keep the friendships you had with the girls in your old school. Don't worry about getting your own 'girlfriend' yet. There's enough to get used to being in a new school without all that!

Heads

There are heads of subjects, heads of year, deputy heads, and the feared or famed head teacher (and don't forget the head lice!). All these teachers have special roles in school. They make sure you all learn and do well. Don't be scared of any of them! Tell them about anything that worries you.

Homework

There's no escape! Homework can be interesting, but it usually takes time. Get into the habit of doing it as soon as you get home and hand it in on time. Leave it too late and it can be hard to catch up. Use the homework timetable on page 62. Homework is a must – it may mean learning, completing exercises or writing notes. Your next lesson will usually follow on from the homework you've done.

Induction day

This is a really important day for you. Turn to page 61 for the induction day checklist!

Journey

Your school journey may be much longer and you're more likely to go by public transport. Allow enough time to get there in your first week. Being late will get you noticed for the wrong reasons. If you are late, give the honest reason why – teachers have heard all the false excuses before. On the school bus, you may think there's no-one to sit next to. But after a few days you're likely to have friends to sit with. The same is true if you walk to school. You'll meet up with others going the same way.

Kit

Remember when you need your PE or Games kit and make sure they are clean enough. There may be some kind of penalty at school if you don't have the correct kit at the correct time. So it is worth sorting out a routine right from the start. See PE and GAMES.

Loos

School toilets are not always the cleanest or most private places in the world! Make sure you discover where they are on your induction day and use them for what they were intended – and nothing else. They are not a good place to hide from lessons, as in most schools they are regularly visited by staff. ("So where is a good place?" we hear you cry. Well, we're not telling you!)

Loneliness

This is one of the biggest fears of moving on. But for most people it soon passes as you make new friends and mix in with others. Everyone feels lonely at different times. But if it really gets bad, talk to your form tutor about it. Many people also find a faith in God a real help when they're feeling lonely. Why not have a look at the Bible poem on page 46.

Maths 4 + 5 = 10

Maths is necessary for virtually all careers, so it is worth working at it and trying really hard. Don't forget that your teacher is there to help you, so ask if you don't understand.

Money

You'll find that you will always feel like you need more money than you actually have. But money is not always available, so decide what you really need and what you don't. You need money for lunch and bus fares, but don't take too much in case you lose it or it gets taken.

New

You will look and act 'new' for a few days. Starting somewhere new does give you a chance to put the past behind you and make a fresh start. If you start really well, you won't have to 'catch up' later on. Your new school is a great opportunity to make a positive new beginning. First impressions are important.

PE and Games

There will be more equipment and facilities and a variety of activities and games on offer. There will be more of a challenge. If you enjoy sport, you'll love it. If you don't, you might as well join in as there's really no choice anyway! Whatever the case, always try and do your best – we can't all be Olympic gold medallists. Getting changed for PE and Games can be embarrassing too. Remember that everyone develops physically at different speeds. Sport is not just for winners - exercise helps you to develop your physique and feel good about yourself. See KIT.

Office

The school office is a busy place, with the staff doing many jobs. Once you get used to the way the school office works, you will be confident about how to use it and how the staff can help you. Most office staff are very friendly!

Opportunities

WOW! What opportunities! More clubs, more subjects, more friends, trips to more places than would be possible in your old school! You may want to keep out of it all for a while, but once you are settled don't waste the opportunities school provides.

Parents

Despite being so old and out of touch, parents do want to know how their kids are getting on. They want you to succeed and be happy. If you're not, they will worry. Try to let them help you by talking to them about the good things and the hard things too. If you are finding it really hard, ask them to speak to school for you. See page 23.

PSE

Personal and Social Education covers a range of subjects to help you think through how to develop as a person. PSE includes health and sex, law and police, and often beliefs. Through PSE you should learn that it is OK to be different and have beliefs that others don't share.

Rules

All schools have rules and sanctions. Most are for the safety and well-being of all the students. You may even get a chance to create your own form rules. Rules are there to follow rather than to break. Find out what they are and stick to them from the start. If you don't, you may find yourself with things like detentions, report cards and letters home to your parents... not a good start!

Religious Education (RE)

Beliefs are a key part of society. It is important to learn about and understand what people of all religions believe and how that affects their behaviour and attitudes. Christianity is about choosing to follow God. To do so we need to know and understand what we are choosing.

Quiet people

It's great that we're all different! Some people seem quiet; others really loud. Many quiet people are thinkers who don't say much but listen to louder people making fools of themselves! There is nothing wrong with being quiet. Sometimes people are loud because they're nervous or insecure. And if you are more of an extrovert, just be yourself. But don't forget to be sensitive to others. Quiet people also make good friends because they listen to your problems.

Swimming

Some schools provide swimming lessons, while others have swimming clubs. Swimming is a great way to get fit and provides opportunities for races and team membership. You may find changing for swimming a bit embarrassing, but once you're in the water what you or your costume or trunks are like doesn't matter.

Size

Look around the hall, full of all the new pupils. You'll see some boys and girls who look almost fully grown, and others who look like small children. Everyone develops at a different rate. If you are smaller or less physically developed, don't worry. You'll have your growth spurt.

Timetable

Your new school timetable tells you what subject you do, where and at what time. It may seem complicated, but as long as you copy it down correctly it will soon make sense.

Trainers

Trainers may not be on your school's regulation uniform list! But they are a fashion statement and wearing the wrong make or the wrong design can sometimes lead to people taking the mickey. Try not to be too caught up by the fashion thing, and be your own person instead. See BULLIES.

Teachers

You are likely to have many more teachers, with a different one for every subject. Some teachers seem less friendly than others, but don't let that put you off their subject. Teachers are there to help you learn, so ask them questions or tell them if you don't understand things. Try to remember that teachers are normal people, with problems and moods just like you! If you want a laugh, read *My Teacher* on page 21.

Tests and exams

Tests and exams are part of school life. As you get older they will help you decide what you are good at and what you may want to do in the future. All you can do is your best. You will do better if you've prepared for them and you don't panic.

Uniform

Your new school uniform may be more formal and strict than you are used to. Schools usually have uniforms to make the students feel united and look moderately smart. The rules will be clear on what you can and can't wear.

Web site

Many larger schools now have their own web sites and many of the questions you would like to ask will be on it. There may also be more up-to-date information than in the prospectus, with news about school trips, sports competitions and staff changes. Web sites are a great way to access information, so it is well worth a look.

Youngest

Being the youngest in school (and possibly the smallest) could make you feel vulnerable and scared. By this time next year, however, you'll feel settled and confident, while next year's newest pupils will be feeling as you do now. Being the youngest does give you more excuses for being late or getting lost on the way to lessons!

Zits

The time you change school coincides with adolescence, when you and your body are changing. Zits and spots are unavoidable as you grow up, but if you keep your face clean by washing it regularly, and eat fruit and vegetables, you can stop them getting too bad. A few people may get them really badly (this is usually called acne) but your doctor should be able to offer some help if this is the case.

Top Ten Answers!

781 children in the United Kingdom, who are about to move on to secondary schools, were asked these three questions. Their answers made up the top ten charts on the next few pages.

- What is the best thing about your new school?
- What will you miss most of all about your old school?
- What is the most scary thing about your new school?

How would you answer these questions? Turn over to see if your answers are in the Top Ten! Here are comments from three children in Bolton.

"On the visit, I liked my form tutor and getting things to do in geography. But I disliked some older children because they pushed me in the ice-cream queue! I want to be in the school football team. My dream is to be a footballer." Justin Hill

"I'm looking forward to my new school because it's bigger and it's got more rooms and I'll get a different teacher for every lesson. I wouldn't like it if I didn't make any friends. I'm looking forward to playing either a cornet or a trumpet, and after-school clubs. When I get older, I would like to be a lawyer and drive a silver Jaguar." Chloe Sherwood

"I like my new secondary school because it's got interesting sports. I can't find anything I dislike except for the fact that it's falling apart! On my visit I did rock-climbing and abseiling. That was fun. I also met some teachers. They were kind. I want to become either a policeman, a lawyer or a pilot." Kamran Afhal

Thanks to the children from Balvanich Primary (Isle of Benbecula); Cairnshill Primary (S Belfast); Coppull St John's Primary (Lancashire); Gibson Primary (Omagh); Gilnow Primary (Bolton); Hillview Primary (Hucclecote, Gloucester); Kingsland School (Bangor, N Ireland); Loughton Middle School (Milton Keynes); Mellor Primary (Leicester); many Nottinghamshire Primary Schools who know Nick Harding!; St Anthony's RC Primary (Watford); St John's C of E Primary (Sparkhill, Birmingham); St John's C of E Primary (Brinscall, Lancashire); St John's C of E Primary (Whittle-le-Woods, Lancashire); St Joseph's RC Primary School (Carryduff, N Ireland); St Mary's C of E Primary (Kirtbury, W Berks); Swanbourne House School (Milton Keynes).

What is the best thing about your new school?

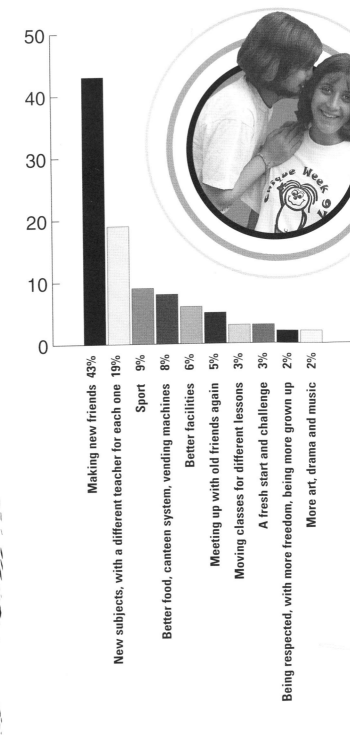

Making new friends	43%
New subjects, with a different teacher for each one	19%
Sport	9%
Better food, canteen system, vending machines	8%
Better facilities	6%
Meeting up with old friends again	5%
Moving classes for different lessons	3%
A fresh start and challenge	3%
Being respected, with more freedom, being more grown up	2%
More art, drama and music	2%

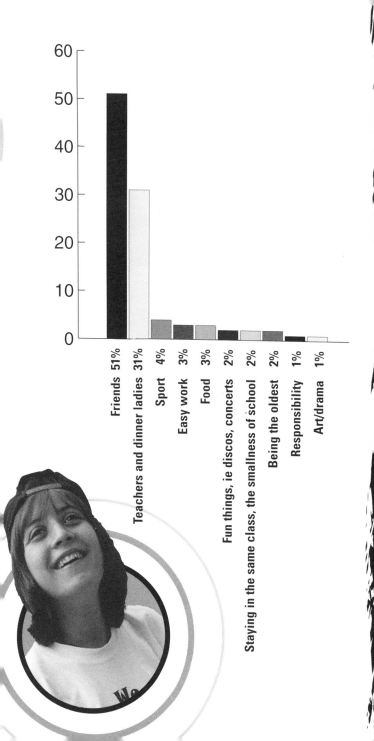

What will you miss most of all about your old school?

- Friends 51%
- Teachers and dinner ladies 31%
- Sport 4%
- Easy work 3%
- Food 3%
- Fun things, ie discos, concerts 2%
- Staying in the same class, the smallness of school 2%
- Being the oldest 2%
- Responsibility 1%
- Art/drama 1%

What is the most scary thing about your new school?

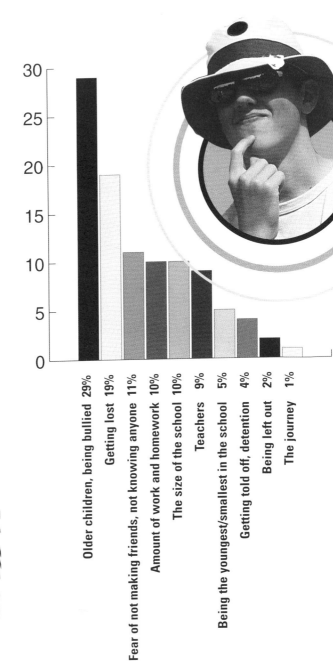

Older children, being bullied 29%
Getting lost 19%
Fear of not making friends, not knowing anyone 11%
Amount of work and homework 10%
The size of the school 10%
Teachers 9%
Being the youngest/smallest in the school 5%
Getting told off, detention 4%
Being left out 2%
The journey 1%

My teacher

My teacher once wore nappies
My teacher used to crawl
My teacher used to cry at night
My teacher used to bawl.

My teacher jibber
jabbered
My teacher ran up
stairs
My teacher wrote
in squiggles
My teacher stood
on chairs.

My teacher once was
naughty
My teacher was so rude
My teacher used a bad
word
My teacher spilled her food.

My teacher lost her homework
My teacher took too long
My teacher got detention
My teacher did things wrong.

My teacher's all grown-up now
My teacher can't recall
My teacher thinks she's different
My teacher's not at all.

Taken from *The Day I Fell Down the Toilet*, by Steve
Turner, Lion Publishing. Reproduced with permission.

Friends

Friends are like fire,
spreading across vast
areas
and reaching out for
everything in its path.
But when something
new and different
comes along – like
water,
it can all extinguish
with one blast
so your friendship is
left as history, as ash.
But sometimes there's
a spark.
If you save that spark,
you can light it again.
Your friendship can
start again,
slowly return to what
you had.

Daisy Shirley-Beavan (10),
from *Our poems and no
messin'*, © Scripture Union
1999.

You're still you

You're swapping your recorder for a rock guitar
You've put a centre parting in your hair.
You've thrown away those CDs with the nice songs on,
And black's the only colour that you'll wear.

You look at me as though I'm sad, or even worse,
As though I'm getting past my sell-by date.
You need me as your taxi-driver every night,
But you don't want me at that new school gate.

But you're still you and I'm still me,
Just two people getting by.
Making our way in this world so wide,
Can we still walk side by side?

OK, so I'm your mother and right down deep
Are some complicated feelings for you.
I want you to be happy and I know I can't keep
You a child for ever. What should I do?

So let me go slowly, tell me I'm cool,
That we're just two people finding a way
To pass through changes in this world so
wide
And still walk side by side.

Can we still walk side by side?

© Gill Saxon, 2000

Gill wrote this when her daughter,
Emma, was about to move to
Impington Village College in
Cambridge.

Come to the edge.

We might fall.

Come to the edge.

It's too high!

Come to the edge

And they came

and he pushed

and they flew.

This poem was quoted by Mary McAleese in her inaugural address as the President of the Irish Republic, when she was urging people to take risks and to trust.

'Come to the Edge' by Christopher Logue from *Selected Poems*, Faber and Faber. Reproduced with permission.

What shall I do?

Help!

Nick Jeffery spends his time in Bristol, 'helping boys and girls settle into their secondary schools'. He's met thousands of people who know about bullying, which is one of the things that can really worry you when you change school. If you need convincing, look at the questionnaire results on page 20. He's worth listening to.

It's funny, isn't it, that staff at secondary school sometimes give you the wrong message. Take bullying, for instance! There you are, in the main hall during your first week listening to a dull (sorry), exciting lecture (oops), I mean friendly chat from the Head of Year. They're talking about how this school has not had an instance of bullying since 1875, but if you are bullied, see someone who can really help you! They may even say, "There are no bullies in this school!" Now that is risky, because if you are bullied, you will think it must be your fault. The truth is, every school has bullies. If you think about it, I bet you've been bullied before. And if you're really honest, you've probably bullied someone yourself too! (Yes, even someone as angelic as you!) Believe it or not, being bullied is not the real problem; it's what you do about it that counts.

There is an unwritten rule in school amongst pupils that says, "Never tell on a bully!" Why not? Who says? Doesn't it just make things worse, mess up the victim's life and make the bully think he or she can get away with it? Or have I missed the point? Being bullied can make us feel really lonely. Some pupils won't tell anyone at all. They just stay silent and suffer. There is an episode of The Simpsons — you know, the one where Nelson is bullying Bart. He is being 'got' after school. He sits in the classroom all day, terrified but not doing anything about it. At the end of school he tries to run away but Nelson is waiting and beats him up. Nelson tells him that he will get beaten up every day after school! Eventually Bart does something about it.

What would you do? Have a look at 'Dilemmas' and see how you get on...

25

Dilemmas

1 Your mate is being pushed around by some big kids and calls to you for help. What do you do?

☐ A Pretend you didn't hear anything and scurry off to your next class.
☐ B Dive in, like Superman, to the rescue only to limp out five minutes later with more than your pride hurt.
☐ C Ask an adult in school to sort it out.

2 Someone in your tutor group has started picking on you and has threatened to beat you up after school. What will you do?

☐ A Spend all day worrying about it instead of concentrating on your lessons, and pray that they will forget.
☐ B Face the bully and threaten them with worse stuff.
☐ C Wait for the end of tutor time, then quietly explain what is going on to your tutor or an adult you trust.

3 Your friend rushes into the tutor group, late. There's a long piece of loo paper hanging out of the back of his trousers. Do you...

☐ A Fall about in hysterics, with everybody else?
☐ B Drag him outside before anyone sees?
☐ C Report it so that the teacher can deal with this serious matter?

4 In Science, you overhear two of your tutor group whispering about a secret you shared with just your best friend. What will you do?

☐ A Say nothing and stop being best friends.
☐ B Make up some things about your friend and tell everyone to get your own back.
☐ C Confront your friend, hear their side of the story, then decide what to do.

5 You find some kids in the toilets, blocking the sinks and turning on the taps. They see you and tell you to ignore it, "or else!". Do you...

☐ A Ignore it?
☐ B Stop the flood by unblocking the sinks yourself?
☐ C Find an adult immediately?

How did you get on?

Mostly A – OK, so you like to play it safe, but watch out. You may become a doormat or you could be in danger of being bullied yourself. You have rights and are special. Try to be more like C.

Mostly B – Woah! You throw caution to the wind and get stuck in there. Slow down, take a deep breath and think before you act or you could find yourself in big trouble at school.

Mostly C – You're not scared to speak out about what's going on around you. Once a bully sees you can't be intimidated, they'll soon give up. But you don't have to report everything to a teacher. Some things you can deal with yourself - like stray loo paper!

Sophie Friend had mixed feelings about going up to secondary school. "I was scared that I might not make any friends and that I'd get bullied, though I was excited too because it was such a big step in my life."

So, how did Sophie survive? Did she make friends? You bet she did. Her social diary is currently booked solid and she's having the best time ever!

Geoff Miller thought he'd keep getting lost when he started senior school. It was humungous; ten times bigger than his primary school: "It was like a maze. Endless corridors, hundreds of rooms, thousands of people."

"But it was fine because in Year 7 all my lessons were in the same rooms. I never got lost once. And now I know my way around the whole school."

Danielle Wade was worried about her speling, sorry, spelling! She thought the teechers would get mad at her for making misteaks.

Did they? "No, they were really nice. They kept giving me commendations to encourage me. I got bundles of them. In Year 7 you've only got to blow your nose and someone will give you a commendation for it. But make the most of it. They don't bother once you get into Year 8!"

Jonathan Hulin was a bit scared he'd have the mickey taken out of him because he hated sports – all sports – but especially football. Also, because he was tall and skinny, he dreaded the communal showers. He suffered agonies just thinking about it.

"It was hard at first. Some people used to call me names like 'Twiglet' and stuff, but my real friends stuck by me. I played football because I had to but, by the end of the autumn term, I realised I didn't hate it any more. I actually looked forward to it. And now that I play regularly, I'm not so skinny any more. I've got muscles!"

Katie was used to starting again, but it didn't get any easier! See how she got on in these first two chapters of *Liar*, from the *Seasiders* series. If you enjoy them, turn to page 43 to see how you can get hold of your own copy.

Chapter 1

Normal

"What's your name?"

It's a perfectly normal question, but it still made me freeze up inside.

"Katie," I would always say, to give myself time to think. And by the time they asked, "Katie who?" I would have remembered what my surname was meant to be. Katie Martin... Katie Wilson... no, Katie Gray...

The name kept changing, see. It was very confusing. For two years I felt as if I didn't know who I was. And now, when it's safe to go back to my real name – Katie Martin, the one I was born with – I still feel sort of mixed up. Who am I really? Where do I belong?

It's quite safe now. He's in prison and there's nothing to be scared of any more. I keep telling myself that. I keep telling Mam, too... but she still has the nightmares.

"Wake up, Mam! Wake up! You've been dreaming again."

It's really hard to wake her sometimes. She gets hold of me so tight that it hurts, and screams, "No! No! You're not taking my Katie!"

"Mam, let go. Mam! It's just a dream. It's not really happening."

And then, like a drowning person struggling up to the surface, she fights her way up out of the dream. She'll be trembling, gasping for breath. She'll look around as if she doesn't have a clue where she is. (Mind you, that's not surprising, we've lived in so many different places.)

And then I get her a drink and we talk for a while. It's best if she doesn't go straight back to sleep, because the dream can take over again.

"I'm sorry, my love," she always says. "Waking you up like that.

Never mind. Have a lie-in tomorrow, eh?"

"I can't, Mam. It's school."

"Oh, school. Won't hurt you to miss a day now and then."

She says that because for almost two years I didn't go to school at all. Do you think that sounds good? It wasn't. It was terrible. I got so bored just hanging around while Mam was working. And when she had time off, she would be trying to teach me the things I should have been doing at school.

Worst of all, I had nobody to play with. No friends, except the kids who stayed at whatever hotel we were in – and they were only there for a week or two.

Sometimes, if it was term time, people would wonder why I wasn't at school. And Mam would say, "Oh, we've only just arrived here in Blackpool" (or Scarborough, or wherever). "She'll be starting school next term." But I knew that by next term we would have moved on again. We never stayed anywhere for long.

Mam usually found work as a hotel chambermaid, cleaning rooms and making beds. Not the world's most fascinating job – but at least it gave us a place to live, and free meals (sometimes delicious, sometimes terrible).

Hotel staff are always coming and going. If people asked too many questions about us, Mam would decide it was time to move on somewhere else. You can't be too careful, she was always telling me. Don't do anything that will make people notice you. If he gets on our trail again...

But now he was in prison. He would be locked up for years. We were safe, and we could start to live a normal life again... or try to.

We live in a town called Westhaven, at the Sea View Hotel. It isn't much compared with some of the places that we've stayed in, but the people are nice. Mr and Mrs Thorne – Terry and Lisa – run the place. They have two boys. David is ten, the same age as me, and Jake is two years older.

David's all right, I suppose. I mean, he's quite friendly most of the time, except at school. Just because we walked to school together once or twice, people were saying he was my boyfriend. He got all embarrassed and stopped talking to me at school.

But Jake's the one I really like. He saved my life once. He's really brave. He and his friend Neddy rescued me after I was kidnapped. I wouldn't mind people thinking he was my boyfriend... but he never seems to notice me much. (Except to get annoyed if I beat him at snooker.)

The Sea View Hotel is in Fountain Square. "Where's the fountain?" visitors always ask, because there isn't one. What used to be a fountain is just a headless statue covered in seagull droppings. What used to be a pool is an empty circle of stone. The whole area is a bit like that – "gone down in the world", Mam says.

It must have been quite posh a hundred years ago, when each of the tall, thin houses belonged to one family. Nowadays they've been split up into flats, or turned into antique shops. So there are not many kids living in the Square. I vaguely knew Jake's friends, Ben and Neddy. Ben had a sister, Grace, who was my age, but I had hardly ever spoken to her. She spent most of her time with Megan from the Corner Café.

"Why don't you walk to school with those two?" asked Mam. "You know I don't like you going on your own." (This was after David had decided he wasn't going to be seen with me in public.)

"Oh, Mam. I'm nearly eleven. I can cross the road on my own, you know."

She still looked anxious. "I'd take you myself if I wasn't working. Why don't you walk with that girl Grace? She seems nice."

"She's got a friend already – they don't want me. Look, Mam, what are you worried about? He's in prison. You don't need to be anxious, not any more."

Mam sighed. "I know, love. But it's a hard habit to break. Go on then, hurry up, or you'll be late for your precious school."

Chapter 2

Drama

I didn't mind being a new girl at school. I've never been quiet and shy – I'm not like Mam, hating to be noticed. It was quite fun being the centre of attention.

Some people had read in the papers about how I was kidnapped and rescued a few weeks before. They wanted to know all about it. The trouble was, I couldn't actually remember much; I had been unconscious most of the time.

But that sounded boring, so I found myself talking about what I would have seen, if only I'd been awake. "He threw me in the back of his car and drove away at eighty miles an hour –"

"Didn't you try to get out?" said one of the girls who was listening. "I would have."

"Yes, but he'd locked all the doors. I banged on the window, and then he told me to shut up or else he'd kill me. He had a gun, of course." (No he didn't, except in my imagination, but who was to know?)

"Why did he kidnap you? For money?"

"He did it because he hates my Mam. He wanted to get back at her for something that happened long ago."

I told them about how, when she was young, Mam used to go out with this guy called Paul. But he was already married. He killed his wife and tried to make it look like an accident. Then he got Mam to tell lies to the police.

In the end, though, Mam told the truth when Paul came to trial, and he was sent to prison. Ever after that he hated her and swore he would get his revenge. (All this part was perfectly true, by the way.)

Mam felt safe while he was in prison. She got married and had a baby – me – and lived an ordinary life, although my dad didn't stick around for very long. Then, when I was about eight, Mam got the news that Paul was being released from jail. That was when we went on the run.

"Oh! Was it exciting?" said someone. By now there was quite a crowd of people, all standing round me listening.

"Sometimes it was exciting." To be honest, most of the time it was really boring. But that wasn't what they wanted to hear.

"Tell us. Tell us what happened."

I wanted them to go on listening. I tried to remember something – anything – that would make a good story. But then the bell rang for the end of break. A sigh of disappointment went up.

"I'll tell you tomorrow," I said, feeling relieved. By then I would have managed to think of something, or invent something. (Well, not invent exactly. I would use what really happened and just liven it up a bit... I was good at doing that.)

This kind of thing – having people my own age to talk to – was the good side of school. The actual lessons were the bad side.

Mam had tried to keep me up with my schoolwork during the two years of no school. She had taught me all the things she could remember learning when she was my age. In maths, I knew my tables really well, and I could do complicated sums without a calculator. But other kinds of maths were a total blank. What was a bar chart? What did "symmetrical" mean?

Other lessons were just the same. I was brilliant in some areas and hopeless in others. The teacher, Mrs Duncan, didn't know which group to put me in. The class couldn't decide whether I was a genius or an idiot.

There was one subject I always enjoyed – Drama. (Guess what I want to be when I grow up?) One day Mrs Duncan told us we were going to start rehearsing for the school play, which would be put on at the end of term. "Who would like to have a speaking part?" she asked.

Most of the girls' hands shot up, mine included. The boys were a lot less keen.

"Luckily, in this play, most of the characters are animals," Mrs Duncan said. "So it doesn't matter whether they are boys or girls. But we do need a few boys in speaking parts. I want four volunteers..."

When none of the boys volunteered, she picked the four nearest. David was one of them; he looked panic-stricken.

"Today we're going to read through the play, to get an idea of what it's all about. It's called The Enchanted Forest. The part you will read this morning probably won't be the one you end up playing, but I would still like you to do your best. Put some expression in your voice as you read – don't just gabble."

She chose people at random to read the various parts. I was someone called Princess Esmeralda. Flicking through the script, I saw that Esmeralda had quite a lot to say; she was one of the main characters. Maybe, if I read well, I would be chosen to play her.

At least I looked the part of a princess, I thought. My face was pretty enough, and I had long, wavy hair which was mostly blonde. (My natural hair colour is brown – Mam used to dye it when we were in hiding, as a sort of disguise. There was no need for that now, but the blonde bits were still growing out.)

When it was my turn to read, I put on the posh voice that I had learned from listening to rich people in hotels.

"Servants! Bring me my fur-lined robe and my second-best crown. At once, I say! What do you mean by keeping me waiting?"

Some people giggled, but Mrs Duncan stopped them. "That was very good, Katie. You remembered what I said about using expression in your voice. Carry on."

My next bit was less successful. I said a word wrong. It was the word consider. "I consider that a very foolish remark." I said the word as if it rhymed with outsider. Mrs Duncan corrected me; I felt embarrassed.

A few minutes later it happened again. This time the word monarch tripped me up. I said it as if it should rhyme with march. Well, how was I to know? I hadn't read aloud to anyone for ages.

It wasn't that I was a bad reader. Reading was one way to pass the time when we were in hiding; I often tried to lose myself in a book. (If there were any around, that is. It's amazing how many hotels seem to think their customers can't read.) But when I came to a word I didn't know, reading alone while Mam was at work, I had nobody to ask about it. I just had to guess, or skip over it and carry on.

How many other words were waiting to trip me up? How many times would Mrs Duncan have to correct me? I began to lose confidence. I started to mumble my words, so that if I did make a mistake nobody would hear.

Mrs Duncan looked as if she was going to say something; then she changed her mind. I struggled through to the end of the play, knowing that I would never get a main part now. I would end up being a tortoise or something, with about two lines to say. Or a tree, with no lines at all.

I felt miserable as I walked home that day. To take my mind off things, I let my thoughts slide off into a day-dream. It was the day of the play, and everyone was panicking, because Princess Esmeralda hadn't arrived. She had been taken ill with food-poisoning.

"What on earth can we do? We can't perform the play without her. Nobody else knows her lines."

Then (in the day-dream) I stepped forward. "I do. I know all the lines." And I proved it by reciting them, word-perfect.

Everyone looked at me doubtfully. "You really think you can do it, Katie?" asked the teacher.

"Of course."

And I amazed them all with my performance. I was much better than the girl who'd been chosen for the part. At the end everyone clapped and cheered and shouted my name...

"Oi! Katie!"

I stopped. That wasn't part of the day-dream. Someone had really called my name.

Looking round, I saw Megan and Grace coming up behind me. So far, I didn't much like what I'd seen of Megan. At school she was always trying to get other people into trouble. She had dark hair cut in a spiky fringe above her sharp, mean little eyes.

She said, "Oh look, it's Princess Esmeralda. The reigning monarch."

I tried to smile to show I didn't care. It was difficult.

"You think you're oh so wonderful," said Megan. "You think you're better than everybody else. And you can't even read!"

"Stop it, Megan," said Grace. She was small, with fair curly hair and a face that smiled easily. She looked like the Good Fairy in a pantomime. (And Megan was the Bad Fairy. Why were they friends?)

Megan glared at me. "You show off all the time. You make me sick. Well, they won't choose you as the Princess now, will they? Ha ha!"

Now I was angry. "I suppose you think you might get chosen," I said.

"Yeah. Why not? At least I can read words of more than three letters."

"I'll tell you why not. Because the princess is supposed to be beautiful. Before you could be the princess, you'd need plastic surgery."

Her fists clenched. "You calling me ugly?"

"I wouldn't be so rude. I do think you should try for the part of the Hippopotamus, though. You'd be ideal for it."

"Oh stop it, both of you," said Grace, but we hardly heard her.

"You call me ugly one more time," Megan hissed, "and I'll smash your face in."

"Ugly one more time," I said, grinning at her.

She took a wild swing at me. I moved aside, and she hit her knuckles on the wall behind me. Now she looked absolutely furious. Maybe I would be the one needing plastic surgery, if things got out of hand.

"What's this? Fighting in a public highway?" said a voice I knew.

It was Jake. He was on his way home from school with his friend Ben, and another boy – Megan's big brother Darren.

"Can't you keep your sister under control, Darren?" said Jake.

"Nah," said Darren. "Mum and Dad can't, so how do you expect me to? Go on, get off home," he said to Megan. "Else I'll tell Dad you were fighting again."

"Wasn't fighting," said Megan sulkily. "She called me ugly."

"So? You are ugly," said her kind brother. "Go on home. You make the street look messy."

EXODUS 2:1-10

Miriam couldn't sleep. It was her baby brother that did it. He was cute,

adorable, cuddly and all those other gooey things, but he was also a boy and Pharaoh didn't want him around. At his first cry or whimper, Miriam had to rush to quieten him. Pharaoh's horrible plan had been to bypass the midwives and order his soldiers to patrol the Hebrew settlements. Any baby boys found gurgling, yelling or simply sucking their thumbs were thrown into the River Nile... and they weren't expected to find their way out. If the soldiers were seen approaching their village she would rush to hide him and do all she could to keep him quiet: fingers in his mouth, Horlicks in his bottle – in fact any of the tried and trusted family methods used throughout the centuries. For three months it had worked, but how long could they keep it up? He would start to crawl – probably right into the path of the soldiers. He would begin teething and, in a land where Calpol had yet to be invented, this meant screaming and lots of it. It was

surely only a matter of time...

Miriam and her mother Jochabed made a decision. Strangely enough, the baby's father and older brother Aaron were not consulted. After all, Jochabed knew very well that the best man for a job is a woman, and so she just got on with things. The baby's father doesn't have much to do with this story at all in fact, but tuck Aaron's name away inside your memory banks – it could be useful. Anyway back to the action...

If the baby stayed, sooner or later he would be thrown into the River Nile. Strangely, the decision Jochabed made was to throw him into the Nile herself. Maybe he would die, but then again maybe the God she worshipped, the God of Jacob and Joseph, would protect her baby. God had promised Jacob centuries ago that his descendants would become great, and that one day God would take them to their own land. Why should her new-born son not be allowed to be part of that day when it came?

She set to work to

make a little boat for her boy. You can make one too. Here's how:

YOU WILL NEED:

PAPYRUS REEDS

(These grow over five metres high so be sure to ask for help when you cut them down)

TAR

BABY

STICKY-BACKED PLASTIC

WASHING UP BOTTLE[2]

1. Weave papyrus leaves into a basket shape
2. Put tar outside (to stop the water getting in) and inside (to stop the baby getting out)
3. Put baby in boat

Easy!!

WARNING

If the boat sinks and the baby drowns either:

a) start again but use more tar this time

   or

b) sell the idea to Pharaoh

Jochabed put the basket containing Moses into the river and

---

[2] The last two items are optional. Stick them in a drawer of similarly useful objects which might come in handy one day. They never will, but don't let that stop you.

watched as the current carried him away. Miriam ran along the river bank, trying to see where the basket was going. It dodged between fishing boats and under the lines of anglers. Once or twice she thought the waves from passing ships would submerge the basket, but it always seemed to bob up again and eventually it got stuck amongst the reeds in a secluded inlet which not many people visited.

Few people hung around here because this was the Royal Bathing Spot, where only the daughters of Egyptian kings could go to swim. A site safe from prying eyes and the intrusive questions of the Papyrus-razzi.

The princess was just going to dip her toe into the water to test the temperature when she saw the basket. What could it be? Somebody's picnic hamper? A mobile home for ducks? A safe place for a Hebrew baby, created by a mother desperate to save the life of her child? Strangely, none of these ideas passed through her head, which was a pity really. If they had, she would have been so pleased with herself moments later, when she took the lid off the basket.

She was about to wade out into the water to explore more, when she suddenly thought, 'I'm a princess. What's the point of having all these maids, servants and under-flunkies if you can't make use of them

at time like this?' So she called one of the girls over and sent her to get the basket.

Miriam watched as her little brother was lifted into the air by the princess. She didn't throw him into the river as Miriam had seen the Egyptian soldiers do to so many other babies. No, the princess seemed delighted, thrilled even. An idea began to take shape in Miriam's mind. She crept out from her hiding place. The royal maids tutted and muttered to themselves. 'Honestly, you find a quiet spot, a place to be alone for a while, and suddenly the place is swarming with babies and children. If you can't go for a bit of a swim these days without this kind of thing happening what is the world coming to?'

'I could find someone to look after the baby for you,' Miriam heard herself saying. The idea appealed to the princess. This way she could have all the pleasure of being a mother, without any of the hard work. The deal was done, and in the first recorded evidence of a child benefit system, the princess even offered to *pay* Miriam's mother for the privilege of bringing up her own baby. (It's a funny old world, innit?)

When he was older and had gone through all the difficult phases of growing up – girls, spots, girls – the princess had him back to live with her in the Palace. Now he needed a name.

The princess thought long and hard about this. It had to say something about the way he was found. There should be the reminder of her stooping into the river to pull out the basket (even though she hadn't... who was going to know that? Princesses could always claim the credit, even if they did none of the work. It was in their job description). The name could be a play on words, reminding others that the basket came out of the river, and the baby came out of the basket. So she gave him a name which means 'Drawn out' (a bit like this explanation). She called him

MOSES.

Taken from *A red sea, a burning bush and a plague of frogs* by Malc' Halliday and Ian Potter (SU). Get hold of the book from the *Bible Bites* series and find out about some of the life-changing things Moses had to go through!

Seasiders by Kathy Lee

An exciting new series, set in a seaside town, where life is not one long holiday!
£2.99 each (+p&p)

Liar
In her attempts to win friends, Katie tells lies to try and impress people. But then she finds herself mixed up in planning a crime and can only escape by owning up to her lies.
1 85999 357 5

Runners
Jake's parents run a small hotel. The new chambermaid and her daughter Katie seem very secretive about their past life and Jake determines to find out what they are hiding.
1 85999 356 7

Joker
Ben, who just can't seem to stop telling dreadful jokes, wonders if his faith is based on family tradition. When his father is made redundant, his sister gets involved with unsuitable friends and his mother becomes anxious, Ben finds it increasingly hard to trust God.
1 85999 358 3

Winner
Spoilt Alexa is living with her strict grandmother while her parents are abroad. Her grandmother does not approve of Alexa's friendship with Darren, and Alexa is humiliated when the friendship goes sour.
1 85999 359 1

Bible Bites
Written by Malc' Halliday. Cartoons by Ian Potter.

A red sea, a burning bush and a plague of frogs
Bite off a bit of the Bible that you might not know, and meet Moses who walked through the sea without getting his feet wet, talked to the trees and made Pharoah into a frog-millionaire!
1 85999 365 6

A tent peg, a jaw bone and a sheepskin rug
Meet Jael who wasn't very good at welcoming guests, Samson who was very good at dealing with Philistines, Gideon who put God to the test, and many more...
1 85999 294 3
£3.99 each (+p&p)

All these books are available from Christian bookshops or by mail order from: Scripture Union Mail Order, PO Box 5148, Milton Keynes MLO, MK2 2YX. Alternatively you can order online via www.scriptureunion.org.uk

Postage and packing rates
Order values: £6.00 & under = £1.25   £6.01 - £14.99 = £3.00   £15.00 - £29.99 = £4.00

OK

– we know that you love doodling on your schoolbooks so here's a place where you can doodle to your heart's content without getting told off. Why not get your best friends to draw a cartoon of themselves to remind you of them when you move on to your next school?

my mate Jo

You have looked deep into my heart, Lord,
and you know all about me.
You know when I am resting and when I am
working,
and from heaven you discover my thoughts.

You notice everything I do and everywhere I go.
Before I even speak a word
you know what I will say
and with your powerful arm
you protect me from every side.
I can't understand all this!
Such knowledge is far above me.

Where could I go to escape
from your Spirit or from your sight?
If I were to climb up to the highest heavens,
you would be there.
If I were to dig down to the world of the dead
you would also be there.

Suppose I had wings like the dawning
day
and flew across the ocean.
Even then your powerful arm
would guide and protect me.
Or suppose I said, "I'll hide in the dark
until night comes to cover me over."
But you see in the dark
because daylight and dark are all the
same to you.

You are the one who put me together
inside my mother's body,
and I praise you
because of the wonderful way you created
me.
Everything you do is marvellous!
Of this I have no doubt.

Nothing about me is hidden from you!
I was secretly woven together
deep in the earth below,
but with your own eyes
you saw my body being formed.
Even before I was born, you had written in your book
everything I would do.

This poem is actually taken from a book called the Bible and can be found in a section called Psalms (psalm means 'song'). Life is like a book, made up of many chapters. In your life, the previous one is about to end and the next one is about to begin. And it is a very important one. You are in for big, big changes. All the future lies ahead. But, at the same time, you can't help thinking about the past.

King David, who probably wrote this poem, knew all about making big mistakes in the past and he knew all about getting worried about the future too. But what stopped him from getting overwhelmed and creeping into a corner to hide was that he knew God was with him everywhere he went and whoever he was with. That's not a scary thought because there was no need to try to hide from God. After all, God knew all about him, even from before he was born. He knew how David would turn out and would protect him. David's life was so full of adventures that he certainly needed that protection!

David was a king who lived nearly three thousand years ago. But what he said about God then is still true! People who read David's songs and poems in the Bible have always loved Psalm 139. They know God notices everything about them and wants the very best for them. It's true for you too, as you begin the next chapter of your life.

When it all gets
too much!

If, after reading everything in this book, you're still feeling a bit stressed, here's a page which will give you a bit of light relief!

There were two snakes. One said to the other, "Hey, are we poisonous?"
"No," he said.
"That's a relief," said the first, "I've just bitten my lip.

What did the plant that sat in the Maths lesson grow?
Square roots!

Teacher: Hands up anyone who can tell me the name of the first woman on earth. I'll give you a clue: apples.
Alec: Was it Granny Smith, miss?

Why didn't the polar bear eat the penguin?
He couldn't get the wrapper off!

Mother zebra to baby zebra: "No dear, we can't afford a new Arsenal strip. You'll just have to support Newcastle like the rest of us!"

How did Tigger get dirty?
He spent too much time playing with Pooh!

How about cooking up something yummy to look forward to when you get home after your first day at your new school?

Chocolate Tiffin
You will need:
100g/4oz margarine
100g/4oz sugar
1 beaten egg
1tbsp cocoa powder
200g/8oz crushed digestive biscuits
150g/6oz bar of chocolate (approx 3 regular-sized bars)
Greased traybake/Swiss roll tin

Melt margarine in a pan over a low heat. Add sugar and stir until dissolved. Remove from heat, add beaten egg and stir well. Add cocoa powder and crushed biscuits. Spread in tin to thickness required. Cook at Gas Mark 3–4 for 10–15 minutes. Leave to cool, and when still warm, cover with melted chocolate or chocolate glacé icing and leave to set.

Be prepared!!

The M.O.U.S.E project!

"What is that?" you might ask! It all began in 1996 with the Bridgebuilder Trust (a Christian charity which works in secondary schools in Milton Keynes). Tim Cutting is their schools worker and he takes assemblies and RE lessons and that sort of thing!

People in the Trust realised that some children needed help in getting ready to go to secondary school so the M.O.U.S.E programme began. A special event on a Sunday was organised in the summer term. People who were moving on up had lots of fun together, played games, did some drama and ate good food. They even met someone who was already at the school they were moving on to (whenever that was possible!).

But last year the Trust wanted to do more. A team of four young people were trained to go into schools to meet the children moving on. They did an assembly with drama and a quiz. After that they did a lesson with each class. Altogether they visited twenty-three schools, did twenty-three assemblies and forty-six lessons! The team also organised a Sunday afternoon event like the one that had been held in other years. It was a great way to talk with the children about what really worried them. After all, it wasn't so very long ago that they were sitting in the same desk as those moving on up!

And have you worked out what M.O.U.S.E stands for?

Moving On Up Schools Education team!

Meet the
M.O.U.S.E team!

Sarah Lynch, Sarah Lamb, Abi Prince and Chris Wilson spent four weeks in June visiting twenty-three middle schools in the Milton Keynes area, to talk about changing schools. Sarah Lynch is a student at Loughborough University. Sarah Lamb, Chris and Abi have just done their GCSEs. They remember that it wasn't very long since they were about to move on to secondary school themselves. After four weeks of meeting Year 7 students, they have plenty of advice!

Don't panic. Look forward to it!

Don't eat too many portions of chips in the school canteen!

Think about how you want people to think about you.

Remember everyone else is new too.

There will always be someone there to help you.

You never get a second chance to make a first impression.

Start as you mean to go on. Once you get into a hole, it takes a lot of effort to get back out again.

Make the first day count.

This drawing by Caroline Preshaws won first prize in the M.O.U.S.E cartoon competition.

From the Scottish Islands

Hannah, Iain and Laura live on the Isle of Benbecula, in Western Scotland. They will be going to Sgoil Lionacleit (Liniclate Secondary) which is nearly six kilometres along the coast road from where they live. In the summer term they spent an induction week in the school.

Hannah Beattie has been to four primary schools, so she is used to being a new girl. She looks forward to having different subjects and teachers throughout the day. She isn't looking forward to getting up forty-five minutes earlier to catch the bus!

Iain MacVicar has an older brother at Sgoil Lionacleit. He knows what to expect. He will miss being just five minutes away from home, but looks forward to the wide selection of food in the school cafeteria. Iain thought that knowing

Jesus would be important if he got bullied because Jesus would know what was going on even if other people didn't believe him.

Laura Whittaker has Down's syndrome and she has a learning support assistant with her all the time. She'll need lots of help at first to get used to her new school. She enjoyed the induction week and after the second day, she was able to go to the bus stop on her own. She made a new friend, a boy who has similar difficulties. She is looking forward to meeting him again and getting to know her other classmates.

The coolest bit of the uniform is the tracksuit!

"My name is James Bruce and I have just finished my last year at Pond Park Primary School. I will be heading off to Wallace High School, Lisburn, near Belfast, in September and am looking forward to starting a new school year there.

What I am most looking forward to is meeting new people and doing new things like Food Technology, Biology, Technology and other stuff that I haven't done before. I'm scared of being the smallest in the school again – in case I get bullied – but I hope that won't happen. There will only be one other person from my primary school in my new class, so I guess I'll have to make some new friends.

The uniform makes me feel like I'm going to work in an office. I've got to wear a tie with house colours on it which I don't suppose I'll wear anywhere else really. I am a Christian, so I'll ask God to help me not be scared."

We're not allowed to wear jeans!

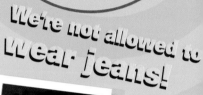

Sheryn

"I'm going to Yardley School in Birmingham," says Sheryn Macintosh. "The uniform is a green jumper, black or green trousers or skirt and a white shirt. The shoes we wear are loafers.

I feel excited and very sad because I am going to leave all my friends behind. But my personality is cheerful, outgoing and determined so I'm looking forward to meeting new friends. I will miss all the extra days off and being able to go off to the loo during lesson times. Changing school is a big challenge but I feel I can trust God in everything I do!"

Homework!

Alex Tang

"I am Alex Tang and I am going to Aylesbury Grammar School. It is very big (that's all I know!). I need to get there on a school bus. Three other people from my primary school are going to that school.

I am really looking forward to going to a new school because I don't like the class I am in now. I would rather have stayed in Year 5 but that's not possible! I won't miss much from my primary school because we hardly have any art lessons (I like art!) and only half an hour of DT.

What scares me most about going to this new school is the amount of homework I heard there will be. When I lived in Hong Kong we had home study every day but I have not had that sort of pressure for a long time."

My sister's there already

"Hi, my name is Joshua Uitterdijk – weird second name, but hey, I live with it! In September, I will be moving to Bishops High School in Chester. Most of my friends are not going there but I chose it because it is very friendly and the teachers seem really nice.

I should know because my sister, Anya, started there last year. My teacher tells us that we will get lots of homework but I know that the amount isn't really frightening. My sister has told me the teachers' nicknames, what the lunch system is, what the timetable is like and what the subjects are. I am worried about bullying, but Anya has told me that they are really strict and work hard not to let it happen.

I don't think I will miss my primary school that much. I have prayed once or twice about getting into the school and my best friend getting in. God answered the prayers, because we're both going to the same school. If things worry me when I am there, I know I can pray about them. And I am looking forward to lots of clubs after school. I want to join the rock-climbing club."

Tim Cooper has lived abroad for most of his life, in Singapore and then Hong Kong. He's just about to start at boarding school, back in England.

"I have just finished my schooling in Hong Kong, but before that I was living in Singapore. The school I went to in Hong Kong was called West Island School; It is an English school, but there are a lot of Chinese people there too. In Year 8 I had a choice: should I go to boarding school in England or should I continue in Hong Kong, after my nine years there already? I really wanted to leave Hong Kong, so I said 'Yes, I would like to go to boarding school.' I also wanted to be with my brothers and sister in England. I'm the youngest in my family, being 13.

I am looking forward to what's ahead at the school, like the rugby and the independence of being away from mum and dad, which is something all my family have experienced. What I'll miss most about Hong Kong will be all the friends I have there. I'm not too worried about the changes going from culture to culture, as I know God will always be with me.'

My brother's coming!

"Hi! My name is Anya. I am twelve years old and I started at Bishops High School, Chester, last September. It is a medium-sized high school and pretty normal, except that it is a Church of England school. Most of the children who go aren't Christians. My friends aren't but they are OK about me being a Christian, although sometimes it's hard.

All the time I was in my junior school, I thought I would go to the high school closest to my home, which is where all my friends were going. But, in Year 6, when we went to look around all the schools, I really liked the friendly atmosphere of Bishops. It was a hard choice to leave my best friends and it has not always been easy for me through the year. But now at the end of Year 7, I am glad about the choice I have made and the new friends I am making.

My teacher in Year 6 was always saying how hard the homework would be and that worried me. But the homework is really not that bad. I was also worried about bullying but Bishops is really strict about that. Sometimes it's hard being the oldest child in the family because I have to go into things first. Everything is unfamiliar and unknown and I can't look to an older brother or sister. It will be easier for my brother, Joshua!

My advice to anyone changing schools is: Don't change into somebody else to make friends. Just be yourself!"

My **mum**
teaches there!

"Hi! My name is Hannah Smith and I am twelve years old and go to Watford School for Girls. When you start at a new school you don't know everyone so you have to make friends. I didn't have any problems making friends but on the first day I didn't know anyone in my form.

My mum teaches RS at the school and is Head of Year 11. Two of my friends have mothers working there too! I think it is fun having a mum as a teacher because she knows what I am doing during exams and also knows my teachers well. If I ever need anything, I can go and see her.

My school offers a lot to the pupils and I enjoy going to Fencing one lunchtime a week. My school is huge and I kept getting lost in the first week, even though I had been there with my mum when I was younger.

My advice to anyone changing schools is: Don't get upset about going to another school as it is fun and you can still keep in touch with your old friends."

What to take on your first day

Rachel Anderson goes to St Joan of Arc Roman Catholic School, in Rickmansworth. This is what she advises you to take on your first day:
"A pencil case containing a pencil, pen, ruler, rubber, sharpener and ink eraser, plus lunch (or money to buy your lunch) and paper, both lined and plain. The teachers will tell you about anything else you'll need."

And she's got some good advice about homework:
"You will get a lot of homework so it's better to get it done the night you get it. Then you get the weekend free to relax."

I didn't get my first choice school!

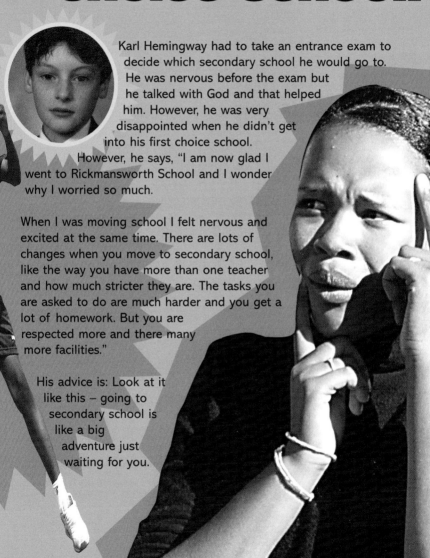

Karl Hemingway had to take an entrance exam to decide which secondary school he would go to. He was nervous before the exam but he talked with God and that helped him. However, he was very disappointed when he didn't get into his first choice school.

However, he says, "I am now glad I went to Rickmansworth School and I wonder why I worried so much.

When I was moving school I felt nervous and excited at the same time. There are lots of changes when you move to secondary school, like the way you have more than one teacher and how much stricter they are. The tasks you are asked to do are much harder and you get a lot of homework. But you are respected more and there many more facilities."

His advice is: Look at it like this – going to secondary school is like a big adventure just waiting for you.

A little love from God

Becky Hancock

" 'Oh God, look upon our school with love, that it may be a place of hope for the fearful' said the small prayer card in my blazer pocket. Very appropriate, I thought, as I walked into the school which seemed bigger than anything I had ever seen before! I wondered if I was in the right place. There were so many children! I just knew I would get lost in the crowds. However, I was surprised to discover how friendly everyone was. They were constantly asking me if I was all right and if I knew what to do and where to go. I met lots of other people on my first day and I felt so welcome because everybody was so considerate. As I left school on my first day my fear had gone; God really was looking after me."

Becky Hancock

In the spotlight!

Year 7 tutor

Name: David Weeks
Age: Middle-aged
School: Chosen Hill Comprehensive School, Churchdown, Gloucestershire
Subject: Geography
Likes: Gliding, ballooning and surfing
Fave food: Strawberries and cream – reminds me of summer days!

Worst classroom experience:
"Telling a pupil to stop banging his desk. 'It's an earthquake, Sir!' he said. And he was right!"

Words of wisdom
Don't believe the horror stories of heads being flushed down loos. They are not true!

Top teacher tips
Make sure you are organised. Then life will be easier for you and everyone else.
Never be afraid to ask for help, and talk to someone you can trust before problems get worse.

Assemblies
I ask God for help when I have to do a scary assembly in front of two hundred pupils. He also gives me the right words to say when I'm talking with someone about bullying or misunderstandings at home. This year in assemblies I talked about street children. Pupils were so concerned, they wanted to know what could be done. We talked about how important it is to know that God cares for everyone, including street children.

Last words
Always make an effort to make new friends. Don't just stick with the old ones.

Year 8 tutor

Name: Alison Woodward
Age: 28
School: St Paul's Roman Catholic School, Milton Keynes
Subject: Italian and French. Currently a Year 8 form tutor too.
Fave food: Pasta with anything (well, nearly!)
Likes: Hockey, skiing, travelling

My first day at secondary school

I had a nice new uniform (including trendy navy-blue tank top) and a VERY large bag! I expected secondary school to be just like Grange Hill on TV and I remember being disappointed that my school didn't have any stairs.

Words of wisdom

Tutors or teachers do actually want to help you settle in – they don't just shout for the sake of it!

Make the effort to speak to the other people in your form group and in other classes. Don't just hang around with those from your previous school. Also, be aware of other students who may have just moved to the area and do not know anybody – make sure you include them.

What not to do!

Make sure you know what you need for the first day. However, you don't have to buy brand new trainers, every type of pen available, all the latest software packages, a new computer, the whole of W H Smith, etc…

First impressions last a long time, so make sure yours are good for organisation, presentation and behaviour. Your aim should not be to establish yourself as the toughest, roughest, loudest member of the year group!

Top teacher tips

This is your chance to make a fresh start – make a stand for what you know is right. Make the most of new opportunities. Go along to clubs and try out new activities.

Don't forget!

There are many people you can turn to for help or for a chat. Remember that God is one of them. I often pray as I drive to work (with my eyes open, I must add!) to ask for his strength and help.

When you visit your new school there are some key things to do:

- Make notes and write down everything you need to remember.
- Behave in a way that won't get you noticed too quickly.
- Try to get to know one or two other pupils in your new form.
- Find out about:

  the layout of the school
  where the toilets are
  your timetable
  the uniform
  the time you should arrive each morning
  where the drinks and chocolate machines are (let's get our priorities right!!).

If these issues aren't raised, ask questions to make sure you know all you need to know.

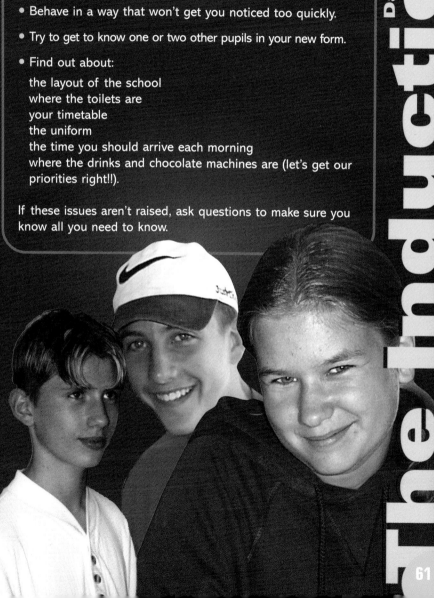

Homework Timetable

Monday	Tuesday	Wednesday	Thursday	Friday

Scripture Union is a registered Christian charity

which works in lots of countries around the world. Christians feel that their belief in Jesus is important and affects how they live their lives every day . Scripture Union employs schools workers who work with local schools to do assemblies, RE lessons and act as a listening ear to pupils of all ages. Scripture Union also runs holidays and camps for children and young people throughout the British Isles and publishes books for young people, including One Up (below). If you'd like to find out more about what Christians believe, or more about the work of Scripture Union, you can contact us at the address below or check out our website on www.scriptureunion.org.uk

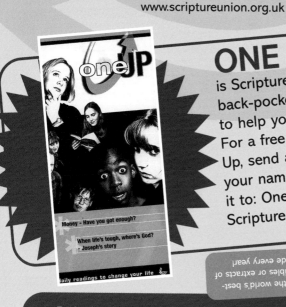

Money – Have you got enough?

When life's tough, where's God?
– Joseph's story

daily readings to change your life

ONE UP

is Scripture Union's jeans-back-pocket-friendly guide to help you read the Bible. For a free sample of One Up, send a postcard with your name and address on it to: One Up Free Sample, Scripture Union (address below).

Answer from p6: The Bible is the world's best-selling book. Over 500 million Bibles or extracts of the Bible are distributed worldwide every year!

England and Wales: Scripture Union, 207–209 Queensway, Bletchley, Milton Keynes, MK2 2EB, England. Tel: 01908 856000
Northern Ireland: Scripture Union, 157 Albertbridge Road, Belfast, Northern Ireland, BT5 4PS. Tel: 0 28 9045 4806
Republic of Ireland: Scripture Union, 87 Lower George's Street, Dun Laoghaire Co, Dublin, Irish Republic. Tel: 0 1 280 2300
Scotland: Scripture Union, 9 Canal St, Glasgow, G4 0AB. Tel: 0141 332 1162

Nick's Last Words for
Survival

1 ## Preparation

Make sure you take all the equipment you need every day (the My Little Pony lunchbox you had at primary school may need updating!). Have a notebook to jot down important info about school. Check your travel arrangements – walking, cycling, car, bus, helicopter - **BE SAFE.**

2 ## Punctuality

Arrive on time every morning (preferably alert after a good night's sleep). Carry a timetable with you at all times so you know which class you're supposed to be in and when. This will avoid major embarrassment!

3 ## Perspective

Secondary school isn't really a 'wild jungle' – more like a zoo with lots of interesting animals, so don't hide behind the friends you already know; make some new ones. The zoo keepers are there to help you, not just to contain you – don't be afraid to ask if you need anything. Beware, there are a few dangerous species (but even they are in cages!).

Nick Jeffery spent three years as a Community Worker with the Royal Navy. He has 12 years of experience as a Christian schools worker. He now sets up projects with the local authority to support pupils who are in their first year at secondary school. He is married with three children and is a mad supporter of Portsmouth Football Club!